Cute Animals of the Wild

CLEVER READERS

Table of Contents

Deer

The deer species has been around for millions of years. There is about 90 different species of the deer and they belong to the family of, Cervidae. Animals like the moose, elk and caribou are also a part of this family. Deer are considered ruminants. This means they chew their food, swallow it, then bring it back up to chew again - like a cow. In this article we are going to discover many more facts about the deer species. So let's get started.

A Deer's Antlers

Did you know the male deer has antlers and the female reindeer has them, too? Antlers are not horns. These bony formations grow from the deer's head. They can be very large and impressive. New antlers are covered in fine hairs called, velvet. After time, the soft velvet wears off.

Baby Deer

Did you know a fawn is born with white spots on its body? These spots keep the baby deer safe, by helping it blend in with its surroundings. The fawn can weigh from 4 to 8 pounds and will suckle milk from its mother. A fawn learns to stand and walk quickly after it is born.

Orangutans

The orangutan is not a monkey, it is an ape. The name of the orangutan is from the Malay and Indonesian words. Orang means "person" and hutan means "forest," so the orangutan literally means, person of the forest. This animal is highly intelligent and can even learn how to use "tools." If you think all this is fascinating, then check out the rest of these cool facts. Let's explore the world of the orangutan to see what other interesting things we can dig up.

The Orangutan Baby

Did you know the baby orangutan can weigh about 3.3 pounds at birth? The infant is totally dependant on its mother. It is so weak, it cannot even lift up its own head. Soon after the infant is born, mom will clean it up and begin to feed it. The baby has large eyes and very thin arms and legs. It is covered with thin hair and has no teeth.

Orangutans at Rest

Did you know even the male orangutan builds a nest? All orangutans build nests at night to sleep in. This process only takes about 5 minutes. The nest will be high up in a tree and strong enough to support the weight of the animal. Each night the orangutan builds a new nest to sleep in.

Sea Otters

Sea otters are related to weasels. They are in the Mustelidae family and the biggest animal in this category. Other animals in this family include the badgers, wolverines and polecats. This animal is a favorite at many zoos and marine parks because of its playful and whimsical nature. It is thought the otter has been around for about 5 million years. If you think these facts are cool, you "otter" read on to discover more about this interesting animal.

Sea Otters at Rest and

Did you know the sea otter likes to slide? When in zoos or marine exhibits you may notice the otters running and sliding. This is a form of play. In the wild, otters will sleep and rest in a group. This is called, a raft. Sea otters in large groups may hold each other's front paws while floating on their backs.

Baby Sea Otters

Did you know baby sea otter is called, a pup?
The pup looks like a fuzzy little ball when it is
born. The hair on it is very dense and helps it
float. The pup will ride around on its mother's
chest and belly when she is floating. It nurses
milk from her, which is very high in fat.

Parrots

Parrots are beautiful birds. There is around 372 different species. The first parrots date back millions of years. Today, many species of parrots have been domesticated and kept as pets. These birds can make wonderful companions; however, some species are being taken from the wild to put into the pet trade. This is dangerous to the bird. What else can we discover about the parrot? Read on to explore more fun facts about these remarkable creatures.

The Parrot's Nest

Did you know some parrots nest on the ground? Parrots do not build nests in the branches of trees. Parrots nest inside the hollow of a tree in the wild and in a nesting box in captivity. When parrots nest on the ground, they dig out a hollow in the earth.

What a Parrot Eats

Did you know the diet of a parrot varies? Parrots will eat insects, nectar, various seeds and nuts, fruit, buds and other plant material. These birds use their strong jaws to crush the seeds and nuts. Some species of parrots also eat clay for its minerals and to absorb toxins in its stomach.

Kangaroos

The kangaroos is a marsupial. It belongs to the family of 'Macropods.' Translated this means, "big foot." There are over 60 different species of kangaroos and their close relatives. The eastern gray kangaroo is the most common of them all. The kangaroo dates back millions of years. In fact, a fossil found shows one species may have stood 10 feet tall! In this article we are going to explore all things kangaroo, so let's jump right in.

Kangaroo Talk

Did you know kangaroos communicate through noise and sound? This animal will thump its powerful feet on the ground when it sees a predator coming. This alerts the mob to be on the look out. Kangaroos are also able to make hissing noises, coughing, clicking and grunting sounds. These are done when the kangaroo is angry, stressed and calm.

The Eastern Gray Kangaroo

This is the most common type of kangaroo. The eastern gray can measure 10 feet from nose to tail and weigh around 145 pounds. It is grey in color with a lighter underside. It also has a very long tail. It measures almost 4 feet long! This kangaroo lives in the southern and eastern parts of Australia.

Panda Bears

Panda bears are probably the most recognizable of all the bear species. It has been used as the face and mascot of conservation for many years. The panda bear is highly threatened in the wild. There is thought to be less than 1,600 of these cute bears left in the wild. Habitat loss and poor breeding skills is lowering the numbers of this species. Let's explore some more interesting facts about the amazing panda bear.

The Size of the Panda

Did you know the panda bear is about the size of the black bear? Panda's measure anywhere from 2 to 3 feet at the shoulder (when it is standing on all four legs). It can measure 4 to 6 feet long. Males weigh in at 250 pounds, while females are around 220 pounds.

What a Panda Eats

Did you know the panda bear eats mostly bamboo? This species of bear lives only on arrow and umbrella bamboo. Because bamboo is low in nutrition, the panda has to eat a lot of it - up to 40 pounds a day! The panda can spend around 12 hours a day munching on bamboo.

Giraffes

The Giraffe is the tallest land mammal on earth and the biggest animal that is considered a ruminant. Like a cow, the giraffe chews its cud and also has four compartments in its stomach. There are 9 subspecies of the giraffe. The West African giraffe and the Ugandan giraffe are both on the endangered list. This is due to their habitat loss and to poaching. You can see giraffes at zoos and in some protected parks.

The Heart of a Giraffe

Did you know the giraffe has a huge heart? The human heart is only about the size of our fist. The giraffe's heart measures about 2 feet long. It can weigh up to a whopping 25 pounds! Since the giraffe is so big, it takes a big muscle to pump blood throughout its huge body!

Life of a Giraffe

Did you know the giraffe can live to be around 25 years old? Even though the habitat of the giraffe is shrinking, they still manage to survive in the wild. Giraffes in captivity (like zoos or animal preserves) can live to be a lot older. This is because the giraffe is protected from predators.

Koalas

The Koala is not a bear. It is a marsupial, like a kangaroo. It got its name from early settlers that thought this fluffy mammal looked like a bear. The word "koala" is an aboriginal word meaning "no drink." There are 2 species of the koala; the northern and southern. Its closest relative is the wombat. Millions of years ago there were koala-like animals. In fact, there was around 12 different species, but they are now all extinct.

Koala Talk

Did you know koalas can communicate? Males use a loud bellowing sound to let other koalas know where it is and to defend its territory. Mother koalas will make soft humming, grunts and clicking noises to talk to their babies. All koalas when frightened make a loud shrieking sound, as well as shaking.

Life of a Koala

Did you know the koala can live to be around 18 years old? Since the habitat of the koala is shrinking and they have many predators, some of the koalas do not live past being a baby. The koala's natural habitat is now being protected and many zoos have taken in abandoned or injured koalas.